# Mambas

by Colleen Sexton

BELLWETHER MEDIA · MINNEAPOLIS, MN

Note to Librarians, Teachers, and Parents:

**Blastoff! Readers** are carefully developed by literacy experts and combine standards-based content with developmentally appropriate text.

**Level 1** provides the most support through repetition of high-frequency words, light text, predictable sentence patterns, and strong visual support.

**Level 2** offers early readers a bit more challenge through varied simple sentences, increased text load, and less repetition of high-frequency words.

**Level 3** advances early-fluent readers toward fluency through increased text and concept load, less reliance on visuals, longer sentences, and more literary language.

**Level 4** builds reading stamina by providing more text per page, increased use of punctuation, greater variation in sentence patterns, and increasingly challenging vocabulary.

**Level 5** encourages children to move from "learning to read" to "reading to learn" by providing even more text, varied writing styles, and less familiar topics.

Whichever book is right for your reader, Blastoff! Readers are the perfect books to build confidence and encourage a love of reading that will last a lifetime!

This edition first published in 2010 by Bellwether Media, Inc.

No part of this publication may be reproduced in whole or in part without written permission of the publisher. For information regarding permission, write to Bellwether Media, Inc., Attention: Permissions Department, 5357 Penn Avenue South, Minneapolis, MN 55419.

Library of Congress Cataloging-in-Publication Data

Sexton, Colleen.
 Mambas / by Colleen Sexton.
   p. cm. – (Blastoff! readers. Snakes alive!)
 Summary: "Simple text and full-color photography introduce beginning readers to mambas. Developed by literacy experts for students in kindergarten through third grade"–Provided by publisher.
 Includes bibliographical references and index.
 ISBN 978-1-60014-317-5 (hardcover : alk. paper)
 1. Mambas–Juvenile literature.  I. Title.
 QL666.O64S4918 2010
 597.96'4–dc22

                    2009037750

Text copyright © 2010 by Bellwether Media, Inc.
Printed in the United States of America, North Mankato, MN.

010110     1149

# Contents

Mambas are **poisonous** snakes. They have smooth skin covered with **scales**. There are both green and black mambas.

Green mambas
have bright green
skin. Black mambas
are not black.
They are brown or
gray. Their name
comes from the
black color inside
their mouths.

Mambas are long snakes.
Black mambas can grow as long
as 14 feet (4.3 meters).

Green mambas grow 5 to 9 feet (1.5 to 2.7 meters) long. Their long tails help them balance when they move through tree branches.

= areas where mambas live

Mambas live in Africa. Black mambas and green mambas live in different **habitats**.

Black mambas slide through **savannas**. They live in **burrows**, in tree stumps, and between rocks.

Green mambas live in trees in **tropical rain forests**. They hide among leaves and branches.

Hundreds of green mambas
can live in a small area.
Sometimes five live in one tree!

Mambas have large eyes. They can see better than most snakes. Mambas use their sight to hunt for food.

Mambas also
stick out their
forked tongues to
smell when they
hunt. They pick
up the scent of
squirrels, birds,
and other **prey**.

Mambas bite their prey with sharp, hollow **fangs**. A poison called **venom** flows through the fangs and into a bite.

Mambas have powerful venom. A drop can kill prey in minutes.

Mambas stretch
their jaws wide
to swallow their
prey whole.

Mambas have a **windpipe** that goes from their throat to their mouth. The windpipe allows them to breathe while they swallow.

Mambas are the fastest snakes in the world. They use their speed to escape danger.

Black mambas can travel 12 miles (20 kilometers) per hour. That is twice as fast as most other snakes!

Black mambas attack if they cannot escape. They flatten their necks and raise the front of their bodies off the ground.

They hiss and open their jaws wide to show their black mouths. Animals know to get away before the mamba strikes!

# Glossary

**burrow**—a hole or tunnel in the ground made by an animal

**fangs**—sharp, curved teeth; mambas have hollow fangs through which venom can move into a bite.

**habitat**—the natural surroundings in which an animal lives

**poisonous**—able to kill or harm with a poison; the venom that a mamba makes is a poison.

**prey**—an animal hunted by another animal for food

**savanna**—flat, grassy land with few trees

**scales**—small plates of skin that cover and protect a snake's body

**tropical rain forest**—a thick jungle with tall trees where a lot of rain falls; tropical rain forests are in hot areas of the world near the equator.

**venom**—a poison that some snakes make; mamba venom is deadly.

**windpipe**—a tube for breathing air that connects to the lungs; a mamba's windpipe lets it breathe while it is swallowing prey.

# To Learn More

## AT THE LIBRARY

Fiedler, Julie. *Mambas*. New York, N.Y.: PowerKids Press, 2008.

Gibbons, Gail. *Snakes*. New York, N.Y.: Holiday House, 2007.

Gunzi, Christiane. *The Best Book of Snakes*. New York, N.Y.: Kingfisher, 2003.

## ON THE WEB

Learning more about mambas is as easy as 1, 2, 3.

1. Go to www.factsurfer.com.

2. Enter "mambas" into the search box.

3. Click the "Surf" button and you will see a list of related Web sites.

With factsurfer.com, finding more information is just a click away.

# Index

The images in this book are reproduced through the courtesy of: Lynn. M. Stone/naturepl.com, front cover, p. 7; Juan Martinez, pp. 4-5, 10; Maik Dobiey, pp. 5 (small), 8-9, 16-17, 21; Johan Marais, pp. 6, 20; Jon Eppard, p. 8 (small); Michael D. Kern/naturepl.com, p. 11; Gregory Dimijian/Science Photo Library, pp. 12-13; EcoPrint, p. 13 (small); ZSSD/Minden Pictures, pp. 14-15; Robert Pickett, p. 16 (small); blickwinkel/Alamy, pp. 18-19.